FLORENZ ZIEGFELD

Twentieth-Century Showman

BY ROBERT H. BADRIG

SamHar Press

Division of Story House Corp.

D. Steve Rahmas, *A. B., J. D., Columbia U., Editor*

Compiled with the assistance of the Research Staff
of SamHar Press.

SamHar Press
Charlotteville, N.Y. 12036
A Division of Story House Corp.

1972

Badrig, Robert H.
    Florenz Ziegfeld, 20th Century Showman. Charlotteville,
N.Y., Story House Corp. (SamHar Press), 1972.

        27 p. 22 cm. (Outstanding Personalities, no. 37)
        Bibliography: p. 27

        1. Ziegfeld, Florenz 1869–1932. 2. Vaudeville (Series)
Outstanding Personalities)   I, t

    E748.Z5.B3   927.92
    PN 2287.Z5 B3x

FLORENZ ZIEGFELD

Twentieth-Century Showman

His performers called him "a most charming man," "an extravagant producer," "the most spectacular showman"; but his performers may have been biased. What did the public think of Florenz Ziegfeld? There can be no doubt about that. Ziegfeld, at the height of his career, had all of America on its collective knee, paying homage to Beauty. Beauty personified, Beauty glorified: Beauty, the American girl.

He placed that girl on a pedestal, but when he made her walk across the stage there wasn't a woman in the audience who didn't envy her; there wasn't a man, from the gallery to the pit, who hadn't some designs on her. Some, the pure in heart, wanted to wrap her up and take her home to mama; others couldn't help crying out loud, "Oh, Mama, buy me that!"

However, it was not his eye for feminine beauty alone that earned Ziegfeld his renown. He had an ear for the excellent in music, and a sense of humor that knew how to tickle the American rib. His ear for music made him hire the musical greats of the day, from Victor Herbert to Gene Buck. His sense of humor could appreciate the droll witticisms of Will Rogers with his topical comments and Fanny Brice as she pranced around singing "Oy, I'm an Indian!"

What was Florenz Ziegfeld as an artist of the theatre? There can be little doubt about his art. He was esteemed by his contemporaries as a supreme artist and placed in the same class as Michelangelo and Rembrandt--except that he did not deal with such inanimate things as paint and canvas. His was the most perishable commodity, human life itself. He took that life at its best, combined it with the song of the heart and the humor of everyday life. He magnified his productions with the bloom of life at its perfection, he enhanced it so that his vision of beauty became the vision of all America and, through the medium of motion pictures, the vision of the entire world.

How could he do it so consistently? Let us remember the man was an artist, one who never relaxed, and one who never spared himself in the extravaganzas he produced. He had a vision and to that vision he was true. In a word, Ziegfeld lived up to his own concept of the Beau Ideal.

Western Union was a godsend to Ziegfeld. It is quite likely that he was their best customer; he didn't have to be out of the same building before he would send someone a telegram. Even at rehearsal time, when he would be sitting at the back of the orchestra, his comments and criticisms regarding the show were turned into many long pages of the telegram. If he began with, "Now I don't want to annoy you. . ." or "Now this closes the incident. . ." this was a sure sign of a coming deluge. The telegram that he sent to Fanny Brice when she left to have her first baby was a classic of denunciation. "How can you do this to me?" Afterward he wanted Fanny's husband to agree to a certain clause in the contract whereby the husband would limit his husbandly duties so that there would be no interruptions during the run of the *Follies*.

He had a sense of humor which enabled him to appreciate the droll whimsicality of Will Rogers, who spoke of Ziegfeld's plight and the trials he had to endure. "Every time we go on tour," said the cowboy with the rope, "it becomes tougher and tougher for Mr. Ziegfeld. All the millionaires come along and they insist on marrying one of our gorgeous girls. And you know how hard it was for Flo to find them. There'd be times when some of the girls wouldn't come back for three or four weeks." Such was the brand of Ziegfeld's humor. It could appreciate the snake headdress on Fanny Brice and actually relish the way Fanny wailed "Don't send me back to Petrograd," and "I want to be a ballet dancer."

He was born to the unsuspecting world in 1867 and was endowed with the gift for enhancing beauty. He also had that one psychic knowledge about appealing beauty: the world would not begrudge its necessary extravagance.

The boy's father, a dignified man, was president of the Chicago Musical College. Proud as most fathers, it is not surprising that he named his son Florenz Ziegfeld, Jr. But if the elder Ziegfeld hoped that his son would follow in his clearly defined footsteps, he was mistaken. The son had his father's excellent ear for music but there the likeness ended. One suspects that Junior did not always go by the book. There was the streak of the rebel in him.

Ziegfeld made an inauspicious advent in show business at the Chicago World's Fair in 1895. As humble as it was, he managed to startle the Chicago dowagers by inviting them to feel the rippling muscles of Sandow, a strong man he had picked up. The ladies, titillated beyond expectations, giggled, and enjoyed themselves thoroughly.

He was twenty-seven years old on that cold November evening when he found himself in front of the Palace Theatre in London. There was a picture of Anna Held, a girl with a provocative face. She was billed as *L'Eteile de Paris* and her eyes were dark and large. She was a charmer and tiny, and Ziegfeld knew that at last he had found what he was looking for: here she was, the exceptional one, the girl who would be his star attraction.

Her history, as it appeared in the newspapers, had the Cinderella touch. Youngest of seven children, Anna was the only one who did not die during infancy. After the death of her father, a glove-maker, it was up to Anna to go to work and help support her ailing mother. But what could poor Anna do? She could barely make expenses as she fashioned hats and sewed gloves and buttonholes. Yet she scrimped and managed to save enough money for the two of them to go to England. A long time ago she had heard of some obscure relatives in England; now was the time to find them.

She never did find them; what she did find was a job in a chorus line. It was a pity that her mother never saw her advancement from bit parts to bigger roles. After her mother's death, Anna was on her own. Now she could afford to take the long view of her career; she returned to Paris and paid strict attention to voice, diction, and appearance.

Petite and pretty, just five feet tall, Anna had a curvy, hourglass figure. Creamy-complexioned, with dimples on cheeks and elbows, she wore her skirts notably high and her neckline notoriously low. She went in for furbelowed hats; her voice had acquired the naughty suggestiveness of her songs.

"Won't you come and play wiz me?
As I have such a nice little way wiz me?"

For this magnetic creature Ziegfeld had to guarantee one thousand dollars a week-guaranteed at a time when Ziegfeld was flat broke! Curious is the fact that he never hesitated. He fully realized that a star like Anna did not come very often. This was the headliner, the star upon whom he could build his fortune. He promised her the world, promised to star her in a musical comedy, and Anna Held signed the contract. Later after he had married her, there were those who claimed that Flo had only married Anna to make that contract doubly binding. Whatever the truth of the matter may be, their marriage, though ending in divorce, lasted for fifteen years.

Anna had a precious little accent, just enough to make one want to listen, and had a repertoire of songs perfect for her personality. With her come-hither eyes, she always stopped the show when she sang, "I Just Can't Make My Eyes Behave."

The penniless producer made the extravagant claim that his word was his bond, but Ziegfeld lived up to it where Anna was concerned. Anna played *The Little Duchess. The Parisian Model* and *Mam'selle Napoleon.* In *The Parisian Model* Ziegfeld showed how richly he could exhibit feminine beauty. It became a trademark from which he never varied throughout his career.

At the turn of the century Ziegfeld surveyed the

theatre of music with a critical eye. What he saw was not reassuring: Sir Arthur Sullivan's offering, *The Roses of Persia*, with a total of twenty-five performances; *Viennese Life* by Johann Strauss and starring Raymond Hitchcock lasted only thirty-five; Ernestine Schumann-Heink kept *Love's Lottery* going for fifty-five performances. Nor were the comic operas of Andre Messager doing any too well. Altogether it was a fairly discouraging picture for a budding producer.

There was, however, that importation from England which everyone was attending: *Floradora* held its American premiere on November 11, 1900, and it lasted for a magnificent run of five hundred and five performances. It became a hit that established Broadway records. People remembered it many years later as a perfect delight of the musical stage.

Ziegfeld analyzed this success. Leslie Stuart had written the music and the book was coauthored by Owen Hall and Frank Pixely; yet it was nothing exceptional. Its history, back in England, was also commonplace. What it did have was a marvelous thing in that famous sextette. In its American production each member of the sextette was carefully chosen. They had to be exactly one hundred and thirty pounds and five feet four inches tall; they had to be graceful, willowy, and either brunette or redhead. They were to be the perfect foils for the six Gentle Strangers who asked in sing-song, "Tell me, pretty maiden, are there any more at home like you?" But how could one duplicate the loveliness of Marjorie Relyea, Agnes Wayburn, Marie Wilson, Daisy Green, Margaret Walker or Vaughn Texsmith? The darlings became so greatly publicized that they were besieged by suitors and admirers, and three of the six Cinderellas married men who commanded social position and wealth, something unacceptable in the caste system of a narrow world.

What could have been Ziegfeld's thoughts as he contemplated the success of Floradora? There is no need to speculate: the publicity about the girls was tremendous and Ziegfeld remembered that. Years later, he was to outdo that publicity when he emphasized his trademark upon the door of the theatre. "Through these portals pass the most beautiful girls in the world."

One must not suppose that the earlier editions of the *Follies* were as plush and as luxurious as the *Follies* of later years. Ziegfeld knew all the struggles and the heartaches of a shoestring producer. What small success he knew brought little return and less credit from the banks; he had no precious list of angels. His *Follies of 1907* was put together at a cost of thirteen thousand dollars. He could not afford the glittering stars or the important names of the business. While he did have Helen Broderick in the cast, she did not become important or famous until years later.

The reviewers who covered the opening of the 1907 Follies did not have the grace to list it under legitimate attractions. It was buried under "New Vaudeville Acts" and was called "a succession of incidents and specialities." It did rave about the chorus girls who appeared with Anna Held the season before. Evidently, the reviewer felt that the girls were worth some elaboration and he went into graphic details, depicting girls who seemed to be borne on the waves of the sea. And he was explicit about the girls who were dressed as drummers while they paraded in the aisles of the theatre. The reviewer couldn't forget Mademoiselle Dazie who did the spine-tingling Salome dance, and there was mention of George Bickel and Harry Watson, Jr., who already had a smattering of fame. The reviews lauded Dave Lewis for his singing of that naughty, provocative song, "I Think I Oughtn't Auto Any More."

With the public's support, Ziegfeld made the important decision to bring the *Follies* down from the roof to the street level of the Library Theatre. No sooner done than he was to regret it. The box office receipts fell to fifteen hundred dollars; but because he was committed, the producer had to live up to his contracts and sent the show off to Washington. Ziegfeld was in for a surprise: the show did excellent business not only in Washington but on its entire tour, especially in Chicago.

There was no such thing as sitting back and taking it easy; Ziegfeld was planning ahead. He returned to the musical comedy field on January 28, 1908; his production was *The Soul Kiss*. Its star was Adeline Genee, the Danish ballerina, making her first visit to the United States. The critic from the *Dramatic Mirror* went into ecstasies: "Genee is a thing apart; a spirit untouched by her all-too-earthly surroundings; an elf, an angel, a bird, an incarnation of Terpsichore; indescribable in words, impossible of analysis, as intangible as sunbeams..." Adeline Genee did four dance numbers: in an aristocratic Empire gown, in a hunting number with riding boots, a *ballet blanc*, and, last but certainly not least, in a negligee of fine lace and high-heeled slippers.

From the *Follies of 1907* and *The Soul Kiss*, he had enough to plan on the *Follies of 1908*. This time he had Nora Bayes and Mae Murray in the revue. It was a social commentary that took place in the Garden of Eden and the New York of 1908. Naturally there were the girls, more beautiful that ever--even though they paraded upon the stage in an improbable representation of a fleet of taxicabs.

Anna Held was becoming unhappy and Ziegfeld had to do something about that. He made a musical of *Miss Innocence* just for her and commissioned Ludwig Englander to do the score. This proved to be his last musical comedy for more than a decade.

Ziegfeld took over the roof garden possessed by the Liberty Theatre and renamed it the *Jardin de Paris*. Here he presented the *Follies of 1909*, the lavishness of which he had always dreamt and to which he would remain faithful to the bitter end. This edition starred the equisite Lillian Loraine, who had been a great favorite of Ziegfeld. It was Miss Loraine who showed up in an ocean of soap bubbles and she who rode in the flying machine and sang "Up, up, up in my aeroplane." Besides the lovely Lillian there was Bessie Clayton, a pert comedienne. She burlesqued the dancers of London with silk hat and tails.

Ziegfeld's sense of comedy could not resist satire about Teddy Roosevelt. He had Harry Kelly do a perfect impersonation and Harry obliged with all his props, teeth, glasses and "derring-do." The skit called for an African hunting trip. There was a friendly elephant and the lovely chorus girls became giraffes, tigers, and ostriches. Even the elephant was slenderized and photogenic. There was a number about the United States Navy, about a baseball game in which the chorus girls filed down the aisles to the delight of the audience. But the most endearing feature was the Nell Brinkly Bathing Girls.

As an impressario, Ziegfeld could dream up the most fantastic claims about his stars; he really went all out for Lillian Loraine. Since there was no one to contradict him, he did not hesitate to say that it was quite usual for Lillian to receive a bouquet of flowers which also held a diamond ring or a priceless lavalier-- not that the lovely Lillian needed such extravagant boosts for popularity. Miss Loraine had found her rightful place: she reigned as the Queen of Beauty.

What were the highlights of the *Ziegfeld Follies*? What were the flagrancies and the imperfections of his great cast of players off the stage? Couldn't one accuse Ziegfeld himself of some hanky-panky and misrepresentation? Let us remember that the man dealt in illusions. He was completely sold on the lure of female pulchritude and he underlined its accent as early as 1907 with the attractive gathering of the Anna Held Girls. He improvised productions on a broad and lavish scale and created motion picture effects with girls swimming. Above all, this theme brought out Anna Held, the Anna he later divorced.

It may have been nothing but a publicity gag when Anna made the headlines about bathing in milk, but it caught the public's attention, especially at breakfast time. . . "Are you sure this milk is fresh?" a husband would ask his wife. "If it isn't fresh enough for Anna's bath, it's certainly not fresh enough for my coffee." There was even a milk company that sued for nonpayment of a bill. Ziegfeld claimed that the milk was sour and therefore unsuitable for the beautiful body of Held.

Be that as it may, Anna, whenever she appeared at

Rector's or Delmonico's, captured all the attention. She would sweep in with her Parisian gown, cut daringly low; her chapeau would have the most gorgeous feathers cascading about her lovely face. Performing a "scientific experiment in osculation," she out-kissed a gentleman who collapsed after one hundred and fifty kisses. One wonders whether this was the origin of that envious phrase, "What a way to go!"

The *Follies of 1907* had the scandalous dance of Salome as performed by the provocative Mlle. Dazie. It brought Helen Broderick and her flair for comedy to the attention of the theatre-goers. Notable were the songs, "Handle Me With Care" and "Bye Bye, Dear Old Broadway." But that had been only the beginning, and Ziegfeld kept right on with the *Follies of 1908*. He had hired the unknown Nora Bayes to make her debut with her husband, Jack Norworth. She was a hit when she sang, "You Will Have To Sing an Irish Song." Later on she collaborated with her husband and they wrote and introduced "Shine On Harvest Moon." It was to become her trademark during the years that followed. "The Last of the Red Hot Mamas," Sophie Tucker, joined the *Follies of 1909*. The same year saw Lillian Loraine doing her soap bubble number as she sang "Nothing But a Bubble." The lovely Lillian Loraine cruised about in the flying machine and pelted the audience with her flowers.

As a talent scout, Ziegfeld introduced Fanny Brice in the *Follies of 1910*. He had found Fanny at a cheap burlesque house, the Columbia Theatre. Her beginning salary was eighteen dollars a week, her initial song a character portrayal, "Good-bye, Becky Cohen." Fanny brought new life to the old Cinderella story by jumping from the obscurity of a cheap burlesque house into the limelight of Broadway. After her hit, "Good-bye, Becky Cohen," she appeared with W.C. Fields in an automobile skit. Only Fanny could have made the East Broadway Vampire the hilarious thing it turned out to be.

Fanny was called "the comedienne without equal"; yet she could sing "Second-Hand Rose" and "My Man" and it would take no effort at all on her part to turn one's laughter into tears. "My Man" was her special song, descriptive of her personal life. Her husband was Nick Arnstein, a turbulent man and a gangster.

In Ziegfeld's cast there was Bert Williams who had made such a hit in *Mr. Lode of Koal*. As usual, there were many show girls, but it was Miss Loraine in the second act who swung over the audience to the accompaniment of Swiss bells. With the *Follies of 1910* Ziegfeld accomplished what he had set out to do, and he held on to the glamourized rooftop *Jardin de Paris* for another three years. He had established a pattern of lavish success and he clung to it through the singular triumphs of his glorified girls. The word *Follies* had a special significance for Ziegfeld; to him it embodied all the *bizarrerie*, the infractions and violations of human behavior. *Follies* was an exciting word and Ziegfeld appropriated it as his very own. That claim, unsubstantiated though it was, became exclusively his --until 1919. And then it was the little *Greenwich Village Follies* that succeeded in contesting his claim.

Lillian Loraine, the dark-eyed beauty, picked a poor night to have a fight with Flo Ziegfeld. Her timing was very bad: New Year's Eve of 1914. Lillian, who was called "a Dazzler" by *Variety*, was a moody creature and her history with Ziegfeld was one of stormy quarrels and passionate reconciliations, over and over again. On New Year's Eve there was a costume ball held by the Sixties Club at the Hotel Astor. Ziegfeld had donned a tramp's costume and made the picture complete with a blackened nose and a snuffed-out cigar. But Lillian was still shilly-shallying and just before their entrance into the grand ballroom, Lillian made up her mind: she walked away.

Ziegfeld, left without a partner, was on the point of going home when he met Gene Buck, one of his writers. Buck laughed at the idea of going home and talked him into staying. Flo stayed and enjoyed himself immensely.

A reluctant seeker of pleasure! Yet the gods were more than kind. Ziegfeld met Billie Burke, who was at that time the darling of the critics and the paying public. She was not to be stampeded even by such an ar-

sical plays suffered while the revues and lighter,
aningless entertainment sold out nightly.

iegfeld sensed the need for increased visual appeal
trusted Joseph Urban with further collaboration.
ddition to the scenery, he had Urban do the cos-
es as well. At various times and at different shows,
ad impressive lists of composers. There were Vic-
Herbert, Irving Berlin, Jerome Kern, and many
rs. Each had his own characteristic and idiosyn-
ies, and each in his way contributed to the success
e *Follies*.

ctor Herbert, a gregarious man, a fun-loving man,
a product of the Old World and was famous for
mental ballads. Within that tradition and form,
reated rich musical theatre. Ziegfeld would have
the first to acknowledge the measure of his help.
ing Berlin's first big hit was "Alexander's Rag-
Band" and this gave him his membership to
an Alley. He also contributed greatly to Ziegfeld's
ss. He wrote "Mandy" for the *Follies*; Ray Dooley
andy and Marilyn Miller was Primrose, the fa-
minstrel. However, it was not until 1919 that
wrote "A Pretty Girl Is Like a Melody." There-
it became the theme song of the *Follies*.
me David Kern, often called "that fount of mel-
contributed enormously to one of Ziegfeld's
t successes, *Show Boat*.

feld, with his uncanny knack of analyzing the
must have realized that the serious theatre-
uld need something more than the titillation of
es. Beautiful girls were fine; pleasant music,
meaningless, was an obvious pleasure; but could
tre hold no appeal for the intellect?

eld found the answers to that question when
arie was presented in 1924 by Arthur Ham-
. He had been thrilled by Rudolf Friml's score;
ian Love Call" wrought its magic upon him.
as nothing remarkable in the plot of the play;
Dennis King who played the Canadian Mounted
an and when King began to sing with Mary Ellis
e in the audience were spiritually refreshed.
ter, Dennis King supplied him with a second,

dent admirer as Ziegfeld. There was more than marriage to be considered by Billie. She was famous, a
star in her own right. Her name had become synonymous with all that was adorable about the feminine
sex: a dream-girl was a "billieburke"; a fan was a
"burkeite." London had given her triumphs and cred-
its, she had appeared in a play by Somerset Maugham
and was now starring in a comedy; even the newspaper-
men were writing poems about her.

Her producers, Frohman and Hayman, saw the dan-
ger signals and tried to warn her. What could she have
in mind? Of all the men Billie knew, why choose Flo
Ziegfeld? Didn't she have all the college boys cheering
her? Didn't the great Caruso himself show his magnificent presence in the stage box? A relationship with
Ziegfeld was sure to ruin her career!

They had one final argument, reading the roster of
the women with whom Ziegfeld had been involved:
Anna Held, Lillian Loraine, Justine Johnstone, and
many more. However, their arguments fell on deaf
ears. On April 11, 1914, Flo and Billie were married.
Among those present were Ziegfeld's parents and
Blanche Burke, Billie's mother. The newlyweds enjoyed a weekend honeymoon at Long Beach and then
moved into the big house at Burkely Crest, at Hastings-
on-the-Hudson.

The Shuberts, with their *Passing Show,* were Ziegfeld's keenest competitors. *The Whirl Of The World,*
which they presented at the Winter Garden in 1914,
made Ziegfeld sit up and take notice, especially so
after he had read Alan Dale's review in the *New York
American*. "Oh, parents," cautioned Mr. Dale, "keep
your tender boys at home. Keep them, aye, keep them
from the Winter Garden. It is very, awfully, danger-
ous." Charles Darnton of the *New York World* was
no less ambiguous: he claimed it was no place for a
man with a weak heart. With reviews like that it is no
wonder that people came from near and far to the Winter Garden.

There was also that throwaway from *A World of
Pleasure* which the Shuberts presented in 1915. Ziegfeld must have read the reviews with a great deal of

envy: "Perfect from the pinky of the cutest little Pony to the Majestic Battleship." It went on to say how it was the extreme of undress, almost nudity; that it was not for the unsophisticated; that there were scenes in which the chorus wore only a girdle of beads; that at the Winter Garden stockings were as obsolete as the armor of a medieval knight.

It must have hurt Ziegfeld to realize that while the Shuberts were succeeding at the Winter Garden the *Follies* had gone into a decline. Against the daring display of the Shuberts, the *Follies* had only a display of ankles.

Ziegfeld had to call upon names that were big in show business. There was the amiable Frank Tinney who was a favorite with the public; there was Leon Errol who, with his trick knee, had the audience rolling in the aisles; there was Ann Pennington, new upon the scene, but with a sense of timing that was the nearest to perfection. Luckily she came at a time of emancipation: it was quite all right to reveal her dimpled knees.

The book of the show knew the skilled hands of Channing Pollock, Gene Buck, and Rennold Wolfe. Just as important, if not more so, was the employment of the stage designer, Joseph Urban. Urban had studied the methods of Reinhardt and Gordon Craig. He had the ingenuity and the imaginativeness to dream up twenty-one different scenes, giving them all the color of a spectacle, while using nothing but plain colors and flat surfaces. Now Ziegfeld could drape his curvaceous beauties all over the improvised Elysian Fields. The relationship between Ziegfeld and Urban remained a happy association throughout their respective careers. Urban was to remain with Ziegfeld for a long time. Ziegfeld never held him exclusively since Urban was too much in demand to be anyone's exclusive property. Nevertheless he gave the subsequent editions of the Follies the wisdom of his craftsmanship.

Although he was wise enough to diversify his talent, Ziegfeld remained loyal to his popular entertainers. Fanny Brice, who had been with him in the *Follies of 1910*, now appeared among his performers in 1916.

She was hilarious doing a burlesque who was the Queen of Vamps. Also in such box office attractions as Lillia Peggy Hopkins. He also had such tried tainers as Bert Williams, W.C. Fi Cantor. And, of course, Will Roger

In his attempt to surpass anyth could do with their *Passing Show,* Marilyn Miller away from the Shub also discovered a tall, dark beaut name of Dolores. He gave both o arating company of Ann Pennington Twins.

Over the years, Ziegfeld had mar were Van and Schenck, a huge succ "All She'd Say Was Uh-Hum." The ful score in 1920 which included " Victor Herbert and "Girl of My Berlin. Berlin was a modest man prolific, and so popular with the posers of Tin Pan Alley were jea and concocted the fantastic theory boy" made up his tunes for him. advised him to study music ser only shake his head and say th music seriously he might hate th

There was a song which Zieg *Follies,* but the writers, Rodg to part with it. They were ju "My Heart Stood Still" beca number in *The Connecticut Y* not always fail with Rodgers a Wynn in his production of *Simp* of-the-mill musical but it did by Rodgers and Hart, "Ten C

It was the postwar period legging, short skirts and bath of "flaming youth," a revolt was in. Young people could r sweeter music of musical co attuned to the Ziegfeld show citing shows at the Winter more dramatic play when he performed as the *Vagabond King*. This was taken from Justin Huntly McCarthy's book, *If I Were King*. It was a fine role for Dennis King, who became the romantic darling of the matinee audiences. The third answer, *The Student Prince*, was no less important than the other two. This also came in 1924, under the banner of the Shubert Brothers. Ziegfeld could not help but note its musical strength.

Flo, in 1926, produced the *Three Musketeers* with all the splendor at his command. Rudolf Friml was his composer, but for Friml it proved to be his last hit. Again it was Dennis King who played D'Artagnan, Douglas Dumbrille was Athos, Joseph Macauley was Aramis, Detmar Popper was Porthos, while Vivienne Segal played Lady Constance. Percy Hammond had this to say about Dennis King's D'Artagnan: "...he has the voice of a canary, the grace of a swallow and the valor of an eagle." On opening night the show was very long-- not that the audience minded, but it led to a famous remark by Alexander Woollcott: "I did greatly enjoy the first few years of Act One."

But the nineteen twenties ended and with their ending there came a theatrical change that Friml found he could not accept. The melodic airs that soared had flown out of fashion. Now there was a new trend of sophistication in the modern musicals. Rudolf Friml, with his old-world outlook, was too old-fashioned. He was out of the running. In his own words, "When I write for the theatre, I like books with charm to them. And charm suggests the old things--the finest things that were done long ago. I like a full-bodied libretto with luscious melody, rousing choruses and romantic passions."

Jerome Kern had read the Ferber classic and was immediately excited with the thought that *Show Boat* was perfect for the musical theatre. He was in for a surprise: his view was not immediately upheld. The knowledgeable people of Broadway pointed out the unappetizing harshness of the life of the Southern Negro. The book dealt with unhappy marriages; it broke too many conventions and taboos. Worst of all, it dealt with miscengenation. It took the Great Glorifier, Flo

Ziegfeld, to produce the show; Flo's willingness surprised all of Broadway.

One thing Kern did in regard to the musical numbers was to make them truthful to the mood of the play and its characters. It was not improbable for Gaylord Ravenal, the lonely gambler, to sing "Where's the mate for me?" or for the Negro dock worker to dramatize his hopelessness while singing "Ol' Man River." Could Julie LaVerne, that tragic mulatto, better express her feelings than with the song, "Can't Help Lovin' Dat Man of Mine"?

It was billed as "The All-American musical comedy" and it opened at the Ziegfeld Theatre on December 27, 1927. Norma Terris, Helen Morgan and Paul Robeson were in the cast. It was an impressive piece of work, probably Jerome Kern's best. While Kern may have written other scores equally well, this score told an essential story, one that held the power of emotional appeal. Only three years after its first New York showing, Ziegfeld revived *Show Boat*. It was revived again in 1946 and again it was presented at the Ziegfeld Theatre.

The skill was there not only in the combined authorship of Ferber and Hammerstein, but also in the star-studded cast. There was Charles Winninger as the bluff and hearty Cap'n Andy; his wife, Parthy, was played by the adamant Edna May Oliver; Helen Morgan who could be so brave and pathetic as Julie, the half-caste; Howard Marsh as Gaylor Ravenal, who had the dash of romanticism yet knew the hell of loneliness; Norma Terris as Magnolia, pretty and sweet as her name.

Were we to pick out the pinnacle of Ziegfeld's career, it would have to be 1927. The *Follies of 1927* printed his slogan on the program: "He who glorifies beauty, glorifies truth." Although he did not know it, he had reached the peak of his career. It was to be the last *Follies* of a prosperous era. Perhaps he should have been warned by the abundant praise. Brooks Atkinson in the *Times:* "In the art of handling groups of chorus girls, Mr. Ziegfeld has no equal." Percy Hammond in the *Tribune:* "The best of the thousands of revues."

When he tried again in 1931, Flo did his best with a shrunken pocketbook. Although he had Harry Richman, Helen Morgan, and Albert Carroll in the cast, his success was questionable. One could not, however, question his belief in the lavish splendor of entertainment. To the very end he remained consistent. While that may have been the last of the *Ziegfeld Follies*, it was not the last use of his name. Billie Burke gave nominal approval to the *Follies of 1934* which had the backing of the Shuberts. They brought back Fanny Brice and she was in her old form as "Soul-Saving Sadie" as she introduced the first of her Baby Snooks series. Yet somehow the old magic of the Ziegfeld touch was sadly missing. The Shuberts tried again with the Ziegfeld *Follies of 1943* and again they could not duplicate the Ziegfeld success.

To understand Ziegfeld we must understand his competition and we should have some knowledge of what it takes to make a revue. In Paris, where the revue was born, it was given character with social satire and topical interest. With English-speaking audiences the revue had the many additional facets of songs, sketches, low comedy, pageants, ballets and other miscellany. Such was the hodge-podge in which a gradual evolution took place. The world war gave rise to jazz and syncopated music. The entertainment included comedy and pageants of great beauty, which were really a throwback to the older version of entertainment once know as "Masque." During the war soldiers thronged the Variety Halls, and the musical plays of the Viennese school lost their domination. The evolution had taken place: the revue and the musical comedy now held the stage.

Ziegfeld had some stiff competition in revues. Among them was a revue called *Hitchy Koo* which starred Raymond Hitchcock and was produced during 1919 and 1920. It was "Hitcher than ever" and in 1919 it had songs by Cole Porter, while the 1920 edition was graced by the genius of Jerome Kern. This was a formidable confrontation for Ziegfeld, but he was wise enough to know that "if you can't beat them, you join them."

19

He drew up an agreement whereby Raymond Hitchcock went to work for him.

Ziegfeld could not buy up all the others. There was the *Greenwich Village Follies* with its appeal to the sophisticates. Most of it was the lampooning of social and political matters which interested the intelligentsia; yet its producer, John Murray Anderson, was wise enough to know that even the intelligentsia could appreciate immodesty and ribaldry if it was refined enough. Anderson "slanted" his shows to the cultivated taste of his audience. He had found the exact measure of their sensibilities.

The *Greenwich Village Follies* stayed in the Village only two years, then moved uptown to the Shubert Theatre in 1921. Here they had to abandon their original concept of appealing only to the "highbrow" and here, as one critic had it, the show became "uneven and uncertain. . .with dull stretches here and there." What had been a beautiful concept became heavy and coarse. By 1925 Hassard Short had taken over from Anderson. Now the skits had little wit, with the sole exception of a burlesque on *Hamlet*. In it Florence Moore played Ophelia and her Ophelia wanted to drown herself at Mr. Fleischman's Baths. Poor Ophelia had to be foiled, of course, and they solved the situation nicely. Ophelia had forgotten that it wasn't ladies' day at Mr. Fleischman's Baths.

There was the *Grand Street Follies*, also greatly admired by intellectual audiences. It appeared in 1922 down on the east side, at the Neighborhood Playhouse. Its character was plainly written on the first edition of its program: "A Low-Brow Show For High-Grade Morons." It went in for sharp and biting satire; hardly anyone escaped the rawness of its edge. On that list were John Barrymore and Elsie Janis, Pavlova, Irene Castle, Maria Jeritza, and Feodor Chaliapin. They called one man the King of the *Grand Street Follies*, and he was its star, Albert Carroll. He could impersonate the fair sex with a remarkable degree of truth. His Lady With a Fan became a classic. Because of him, the show endured until 1929.

There was George White and his *Scandals*. The

Scandals of 1919 had the format of the Ziegfeld *Follies*.
Ann Pennington with her famous knees was in the lead
as the Jazz Baby. She was a dancing sensation, doing
everything from the respectable waltz to the scandalous shimmy. Neither the book nor the musical score
was in any way remarkable. But who cared? People
had money to throw away. Yet, in spite of its short-
comings, White was able to continue with a yearly
edition of the *Scandals* and stayed in the cast himself
for four years. His show was imitative but White was
contented with his imitations. They were competently
done, and the *Scandals* girls were placed in such
elaborate stage settings that they were more than ap-
petizing.

Earl Carroll began the *Vanities* in 1923 and he de-
pended on girls, more sumptuous than ever. His scenic
effects were overdone, his comedy of standard routine.
He could never develop something genuine or distinc-
tive, but it didn't take much to please the pleasure
seekers of the nineteen twenties. He lavished upon them
one hundred and eight Vanities Girls; he buried them
with a *coup de theatre*.

The only competitors Ziegfeld could not ignore were
the Shubert Brothers. The Shubert Passing Show had
an impudence that was daring, a flavor that was risque.
Their live models came near and nearer to absolute
nudity; their sets grew taller, more lavish, more ex-
pensive. They made the people of 1922 wonder about
the decline of morality. In a burlesque of "The Hairy
Ape" the chorus girls acted and swore like stokers
while Francis Renault, a female impersonator, quiv-
ered and undulated as the Diamond Girl.

And as though not contented with that, the Shuberts
brought out *Artists and Models*, a new annual series.
It was an all-out, presumptive demand upon the baser
nature of man. There had never been so much nudity
upon the American stage. Women paraded about without the benefit of a bra or a wisp of gauze. Their
burlesques and parodies were "the rawest, smuttiest,
most shameless." The familiar runway was forgotten.
The Shuberts favored the steps leading into the orchestra; the chorus girls favored the men on the aisle

seats; the men on the aisles favored the chorus girls. The public raised its moral eyebrow. Chorus girls, show girls, and models became synonymous with prostitutes and whores. The Shuberts kept on their merry way; they had pried open the Bank of Financial Success. One conservative estimate was that seventy-five percent of the audience was stag. Nor did the Shuberts stint on stars. They had Stanley Rogers and Jay Brennan; they had a fresh, young comic, Aline MacMahon.

Ziegfeld met this competition in the only way he knew. He had his dinner-theatre set on top of the New Amsterdam Roof. He kept his old favorites, the standbys: Fanny Brice and W.C. Fields. Urban, his designer, was the best; Ned Wayburn, who staged the dance numbers, could not have been bettered; and the girls were prettier than ever. It gave rise to a declaration which became a slogan: "See New York and the Ziegfeld girls and die."

Whoopee, unlike the exceptional *Show Boat*, was a typical Ziegfeld musical. The book, written by William Anthony McGuire, was based on the Owen Davis comedy, *The Nervous Wreck*. The songs were by Gus Kahn and Walter Donaldson. Ziegfeld produced it at the New Amsterdam Theatre on December 4, 1928. It starred Eddie Cantor.

Here is the story: a hypochondriac, wanting to recover his health, heads for California and takes with him medicine enough to stock a drug store. He reaches our western frontier, stops at Mission Rest and gets involved with Indians and a girl. Along comes the local sheriff who wants to marry the girl, but to her this is a fate worse than death. She induces our hero to elope with her and thus escape this horrible disaster. There is the inevitable chase as the sheriff pursues them until they find refuge at an Indian Reservation. The sheriff loses the girl and so does our hero. In the end, however, he is able to toss away all of his pills.

Corny? Of course. But there were the songs-- two of them Eddie Cantor's favorites, "Makin' Whoopee," and "My Baby Cares For Me." There was also Ruth Etting, and the song that made her famous, "Love Me Or Leave Me."

A curious thing about *Whoopee:* after three hundred and seventy performances, it still played to packed houses. It might have played a year or two longer on Broadway but Ziegfeld chose to close it down. The answer was simple: the great Ziegfeld had gone broke. He had to sell the movie rights to Samuel Goldwyn.

Flo had built himself a theatre, a cathedral-like structure. Joseph Urban, commissioned to do the interior, did his almighty best. The theatre, which was later to pass into the hands of Billy Rose, stands on the corner of Fifty-eighth Street and the Avenue of the Americas. It was in this theatre, on February 2, 1927, that Flo Ziegfeld presented *Rio Rita*.

Rio Rita was not Ziegfeld's best production; it left a lot to be desired. The book was commonplace and had the usual villian, ingenue, and dashing tenor. Yet, it was an auspicious occasion and a day of celebration. Glady Glad, as the Queen of the *Follies*, displayed her fabulous beauty in *Rio Rita*. The comics were such favorites as Robert Woolsey and Bert Wheeler. The dancing was taken over by the Albertina Rasch Girls. It was a new ensemble, stylish in velvet, sleek in satin.

Flo gave the best of his productions in *Show Boat*. When he presented it at the Ziegfeld theatre there was little doubt of its success even on the opening night. How could it fail? Everyone connected with the production had assurance and proficiency. Everyone believed in it, from chorus girl to author and director.

Show Boat was something more than just a musical under fortunate auspices. Hammerstein had done a magnificent job not only on the book and the excellence of the dialogue, but as a lyricist of exceptional sweep and power. Here was the flowering of all the promises to which his earlier verses had pointed; here was their culmination and fulfillment. The boldness and simplicity of the dialogue were "thoughts that breathe and words that burn." He had managed something unique; there was sublimity even in his simplicity.

Hard times came knocking at the door, and something happened to Broadway and all of the entertainment world. In the musical comedy field the productions were more lavish than ever but the public wasn't buying. The girls were prettier than ever, the music was more than ever entrancing, but who had the price of a ticket? For two dollars and fifty cents one could feed oneself for an entire week. The musicals suffered and the *Follies* brought forth no new editions. Flo Ziegfeld and his family headed out to Hollywood.

New York was done for for the time being. All one could hear in New York was that fresh, new lament, "Brother, Can You Spare a Dime?" And how, in decency's name, could one relate that to the lush, plush sets of Joe Urban? Where could you find an audience these days?

The answer, of course, was the movies. People could always dig up a quarter for the movies, fifteen cents for a matinee. No matter how poor, they had to nourish their secret dreams. No matter how sad his appearance, a man could visualize himself as Fred Astaire walking down the Avenue with his spats and cane. So the Ziegfelds went to the movies, to Hollywood--Ziegfeld himself, and Billie and daughter Patricia, who was now sixteen years old.

Possibly the great showman had no real desire for the change. Although he expressed an interest in garnering some of the fabulous money being earned in Hollywood, it may be that his heart remained with Broadway. Not long after the move, on July 23, 1932, he died at the Cedars of Lebanon Hospital in Los Angeles.

The picture of the man remains as that of a dark, saturnine countenance. In his later years, when he had put on more weight, he sported a mustache which gave him a rakish cast of features. Gene Buck describes him as "a. . .quiet, lanky, long-faced dreamer."

At his death Eddie Cantor felt a great and irreplaceable loss. Eddie called him "the most charming man. . .the most extravagant producer. . .the most spectacular showman. . ." And Eddie should know.

Eddie tells of the time of his biggest hit, when he had brought that smashing success, *Whoopee*, into town and Ziegfeld, congratulating him, said, "Eddie, you're a very lucky man! You're a family man with a pocketful of money; you're the biggest hit New York has ever seen. Now you've got everything."

It took Eddie a full moment to think of something. He complained that he didn't have a Rolls Royce and had always wanted one.

Of course, Ziegfeld surprised Eddie after the Saturday matinee. There at the door of the theatre was a Rolls Royce convertible. There was a card attached to the handle of the door and it carried Ziegfeld's message: "And now, Eddie, you have everything. . . Flo."

Flo Ziegfeld was a man born of the great middle class, born with a passion for beauty: beauty of magnificent structure, beauty of song, but above all, a searcher of lovely women.

If we can think of him as Paris bestowing the golden apple to the Queen of Beauty, we must picture that Paris with a large basket of apples on his arm, since the beauties he found were legion.

His was the visual artistry which no one could match. For the perfection of his dream he gambled great sums of money and often lost.

In spite of the scandalous prices he charged for his shows, Ziegfeld was a giver and he gave value for the money received. He brought an awareness to the world, gave it a glimpse of beauty and filled the heart of the world with soaring music. What artist could do more?

Perhaps the biography of this colorful and exuberant man should be written with exclamation points.

EPILOGUE

The *Follies* did not end with the passing of Flo Ziegfeld. They have been resurrected twice since that time. Therefore it is appropriate to review these revivals.

Ilona Massey appeared in the Shubert production of the *Ziegfeld Follies of 1943*. She sang a number that recalled the *Follies of 1907*. "Thirty-Five Summers Ago" was the title of Ilona's song and, like its title, it was filled with nostalgia.

One cannot deny the tug and the pull of nostalgia. There is an aura about our yesterdays which thrill and titillate the interwoven cords of memory. The present, however pleasant it may be, is no match for that precious moment which is gone. Nor can the wildest happiness of the present compare with the despair and the frustrations of yesteryear. And the *Follies*, of course, is in a very special category. How else can one explain the fifth edition of the *Follies* brought back to Broadway in 1971?

Yet, nostaliga in itself will not suffice. Consider the excellence of the *Follies of 1943*, and the equal perfection in the edition of 1971. The 1943 *Follies* featured Milton Berle and Ilona Massey, and made a spoof of Noel Coward's *Private Lives*. In that war year of rationing, the *Follies* carried on a burlesque of a butcher guarding a precious hunk of meat with a machine gun. The production featured the best of ballads, "Love Songs Are Made At Night," Jack Cole in wonderful sequences of dance, and Dean Murphy, who impersonated Bette Davis, Katherine Hepburn, and Mrs. Franklin D. Roosevelt.

What about the *Follies of 1971?* It is so precious that it has won the New York Drama Critics Award as the best musical. It has such old-time favorites as Alexis Smith, Gene Nelson, Dorothy Collins, John McMartin and Yvonne de Carlo. When Marilyn Stasio of *Cue Magazine* saw it at the Winter Garden, she became more than enthusiastic. "The *Follies* transcends the merely marvelous to become memorable."

The secret of these new successes lies not only in their excellence in their own right as Broadway productions; perhaps the single most important key to their dazzling appeal lies in the nostalgia they invoke. It is nostalgia for an era past. The productions may be new; yet they bear the unmistakable mark of their original inspiration: the inimitable Flo Ziegfeld.

BIBLIOGRAPHY

BOOKS

Allen, Steve, *The Funny Men*, Simon and Schuster, New York, 1956.

Cantor, Eddie, *As I Remember Them*, Duell, Sloan and Pearce, New York, 19——.

Ewen, David, *Complete Book of the American Musical Theatre*, Henry Hold and Company, New York, 1959.

Farnsworth, Marjorie, *The Ziegfeld Follies*, Putnam, New York, 1956.

Green, Stanley, *The World of Musical Comedy*, A.S. Barnes and Company, Inc., Cranbury, New Jersey, 1968.

Laufe, Abe, *Broadway's Greatest Musicals*, Funk and Wagnalls, New York, 1969.

Maney, Richard, *Fanfare--Confessions of a Press Agent*, Harper Brothers, New York, 1957.

Marcus, Maxwell F., *Tin Pan Alley in Gaslight*, Century House, Watkins Glen, New York, 1959.

Marks, Edward B., *They All Had Glamour--From the Swedish Nightingale to the Naked Lady*, Julian Messner, Inc., New York, 1944.

Smith, Cecil, *The Musical Comedy in America*, Theatre Arts Books, New York, 1950.

Taubman, Howard, *The Making of the American Theatre*, Coward McCann, Inc., New York, 1965.

Ziegfeld, Patricia, *The Ziegfeld Girl--Confessions of an Abnormally Happy Childhood*, Little, Brown and Company, Boston, 1964.

MAGAZINES

"The Once and Future Follies," *Time Magazine*, New York, pp. 70-74, May 3, 1971.

"Musicals That Were Playful, Irresponsible and Blissfully Irrelevant," *New York Times Magazine*, April 11, 1971, pp. 14-28.